W9-BZB-036

SPECTRUM®

Reading

Grade 2

Published by Spectrum®
an imprint of Carson-Dellosa Publishing LLC
Greensboro, NC

Spectrum®
An imprint of Carson-Dellosa Publishing LLC
P.O. Box 35665-
Greensboro, NC 27425 USA

ISBN 978-1-4838-1215-1

02-005157811

Table of Contents

Dad's First Day

Read to see why Dad is upset.

1 I think Dad is nervous. At breakfast, he almost poured milk into his orange juice instead of into his cereal bowl! Mom doesn't seem worried. She knows why Dad is a little upset. Today is his first day at a new job.

2 My dad builds bridges. Some of them look heavy and strong. Others look light, as if they are just hanging in the air. Dad says the light bridges are just as strong as the heavy ones.

3 Dad is an excellent bridge builder, even at home. Once, we almost filled my whole room with bridges. We used boxes, blocks, pots, pans, and even the dog's dish. It was great.

4 I know Dad has tons of great bridge ideas, so he shouldn't be nervous. I guess he just wants to practice making one more bridge before he goes to work.

1. What kinds of bridges does Dad build?

_____

2. Why is Dad nervous?

_____

3. How does the boy know that Dad is nervous?

_____

4. What kind of bridge did the boy and Dad make at home?

_____

_____

5. From whose point of view is the story told?

_____

6. The last line of the story says that Dad is going to make one more bridge at home. What does he use to make it?

_____

_____

7. Is the first sentence of the story a fact or an opinion?

_____

Bridges

What kinds of bridges are there?

1 Have you ever stepped on a stone to get across a puddle or stream? If you have, you were using a bridge.

2 Bridges are different sizes and shapes. Some bridges have straight "legs," or supports, called beams. Other bridges have curved supports, called arches. Still others actually hang from strong steel ropes, or cables, that are strung above the surface of the bridge. The cables are then attached to the land on either end of the bridge.

3 Most bridges go over water, but some bridges were made to carry water. About 2,000 years ago, the Romans built this kind of bridge. One such bridge, in France, had three levels. Water flowed in the top level, and people and carts traveled on the two lower levels.

1. This passage is mostly about

_____ old bridges.

_____ kinds of bridges.

_____ making bridges.

2. The author wrote this selection to

_____ make you laugh.   _____ help you learn.

3. Think about what you already know about bridges. What are bridges for?

_____

4. This passage tells about another use for bridges. What is it?

_____

5. Are all bridges made by humans? What might a natural bridge be made of?

_____

_____

6. How are bridges with arches and beams different?

_____

_____

7. *The Golden Gate Bridge is the prettiest bridge in the U.S.* Is this a fact or an opinion?

_____

_____

Bridges to Remember

Read to find out what is special about these bridges.

1   Some people do not like to drive across bridges. They look straight ahead and try to hold their breath until they get to the other side. Good luck if those people are driving in Louisiana. There is a 24-mile-long bridge there! It takes about half an hour to get across.

2   If you like to look way, way down when you cross a bridge, you should go to Colorado.

A bridge there stands more than a thousand feet above a river. A 75-story building could fit under that bridge!

3   If you do not like to look down, get in the middle lane of a bridge in Australia. It has eight lanes for cars, two train tracks, a bike path, and a sidewalk.

4   Finally, if you like crowds and bridges, go to India. A bridge there carries 100,000 cars and trucks every day, plus thousands of walkers.

1. How does the text help you understand how long a 24-mile-long bridge is?

_____

2. How does the text help you understand how high the bridge in Colorado is?

_____

_____

3. If you do not like to look over the side of a bridge, why would the bridge in Australia be a good one to cross?

_____

4. Why is the bridge in India a bridge to remember?

_____

_____

5. Name three things, other than cars, that cross bridges in the selection.

_____

_____

_____

6. What do some people do if they are nervous on a bridge?

_____

_____

Moving Out Day

Read to see how Emily feels about moving.

1 *There goes another box,* thought Emily. *All my stuff is in boxes. It's all getting squashed together.*

2 Mom stood on the front steps. "Oh, be careful with that one!" she cried. The movers nodded as they went past. *All my stuff is in boxes,* thought Mom. *It might all get broken.*

3 Dad came out of the garage. "Wow, this is a heavy one! It might break everything else." Mom and Emily frowned.

4 An hour later, the boxes were still going past. One box had holes in it. Emily had made the holes so her stuffed animals could get some air.

5 Finally, they all watched the movers close up the truck. *Ka-thunk* went the big doors. Dad gave Emily a little hug. "One empty house and one full truck. That's a good day's work."

1. What do Mom and Emily worry about?

_____

2. Circle the word that best tells how Emily feels about her stuffed animals.

hopeless   caring   harsh

3. What word best tells how Mom feels? Circle it.

relaxed   worried   careless

4. How do you think Dad feels about moving day?

_____

5. What clues in the story help you know how Dad feels?

_____

6. How do you think Emily will feel when the move is complete? Explain.

_____

_____

7. Why did Emily put holes in one of the boxes?

_____

8. How does the picture on page 8 add to your understanding of the story?

_____

Moving In Day

What does Emily think of her new home?

1 "Emily, would you go turn on the lights, please?" asked Mom. "The movers will need to see when they bring our stuff in."

2 "Sure, Mom." Emily was happy to check out the new house. She turned on twelve lights and then went back to Mom.

3 "Why don't you help me unpack this box?" asked Mom.

4 "Sure, Mom," said Emily.

5 Mom and Emily lifted out shapes wrapped in newspaper. One was the cookie jar. Another was a mug. Then, Mom unwrapped a roll of paper.

6 "Oh, look, Emily! It's the picture you drew last summer!" Emily saw the picture she had made of her family. They were all smiling. The picture made Emily smile, even here in the new house.

7 Mom smiled, too. "Let's put it on the refrigerator," they said together. And they did.

1. Write **1**, **2**, **3**, and **4** by these sentences to show what happened first, second, third, and last.

_____ The girls painted the volcano.

_____ The friends made a volcano.

_____ Bubbles came up out of the volcano.

_____ Baking soda and vinegar went into the volcano.

Some of these sentences are about **real** things. Write **R** by them. The other sentences are about **make believe** things. Write **M** by them.

2. _____ The girls can build a real volcano.

3. _____ A real volcano can be on someone's back porch.

4. _____ The girls do projects together.

5. _____ Mothers help with projects.

6. A mixture of two things makes the volcano bubble up. What two things do the girls use?

_____   _____

7. Who is Mrs. Metzer?

_____

8. Look at the picture. Why are the girls wearing goggles?

_____

9. Was the project a success? How do you know?

_____

Making Plans

Read to see what the Shaws are planning.

1   "Where will they sleep?" Lisa asked her mom. Lisa was wondering if she could fit two cousins in her bed without hurting any stuffed animals.

2   "They'll sleep in the green bedroom, just like last time," answered Mrs. Shaw.

3   Lisa was a little bit glad. "Oh, that's good," she said. Now, she had another question. "What will they do?" Lisa was wondering if she had enough dress-up clothes to go around.

4   "I'm not sure yet. They'll be here for a week. We'll have to plan some things," said Mrs. Shaw. "I thought we might spend one day at the zoo."

5   "I vote for the zoo, too," Lisa replied.

1. Who is coming to visit Lisa's family?

_____

2. Lisa's cousins won't be sleeping in her room. How does she feel about this? Why?

_____

3. What do you think will happen next in the story? Circle the correct answer.

Lisa and her brother will
go to bed.

Lisa will hide her dress-up
clothes.

The cousins will arrive soon.

4. Look at the picture. What is happening in the thought bubble over Lisa's head?

_____

5. How does the picture help you to understand the story better?

_____

Fill in the blank to complete each sentence below.

6. Lisa's cousins will be staying for _____.

7. Lisa doesn't want her stuffed animals to get _____.

8. Mrs. Shaw says that the family will visit the _____ one day.

9. The Shaws' extra bedroom is painted _____.

10. Lisa's _____ have visited before.

To the Zoo

What would you want to see at the zoo?

1   "Is everyone buckled in?" called Mrs. Shaw.

2   "Yes, Mom. Hold on, tigers. Here I come!" sang Jake from the back seat.

3   "Ooh, tigers? You didn't tell me there were tigers there," said Charlie. "Here we come!"

4   Julia was very grown-up. "I would rather spend my time looking at animals that don't want to eat me. I like to watch the owls."

5   "An owl would eat you if you were a mouse!" called Charlie. Julia made a face.

6   "What about you, Lisa?" Mrs. Shaw asked. "What do you want to see?"

7   "Make mine zebras," she answered, after thinking for a moment.

8   Mrs. Shaw laughed. "Zebras, tigers, and owls—oh, my!"

1. How does everyone feel about going to the zoo?

_____ They are tired. _____ They are eager.

2. Why isn't Julia very interested in seeing the tigers?

_____

3. Write **first**, **next**, and **last** on the lines to show the order in which events happened.

_____ Lisa wants to see the zebras.

_____ Mrs. Shaw asks if everyone is buckled in.

_____ Julia makes a face.

4. What does Charlie say would happen if Julia were a mouse?

_____

5. How are Charlie and Julia related to each other?

_____

6. Is this story realistic, or is it a fantasy? Explain.

_____

7. What animals would you like to see if you went to the zoo?

_____

8. What was the author's purpose in writing this story?

_____ to entertain _____ to make you want to visit the zoo

_____ to teach you about zoo animals

Zebra News

Read to learn about zebras.

Where Zebras Live

[1] Wild zebras live only in Africa. They choose open country that has some areas of trees and grass.

How Zebras Live

[2] Zebras move together in large groups called herds. They often travel with herds of other animals, such as antelopes, wildebeest, and gnus. Zebras graze, or eat grass. When the grass is gone in one area, the herd moves to another area.

Other Zebra News

[3] How can you tell one zebra from another? By their stripes, of course. Each zebra's stripes are different from every other zebra's stripes. The animals' stripes help them blend together when they are in a herd. That makes it harder for lions to single out and catch one zebra.

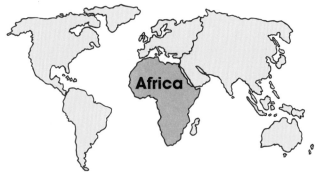

1. What is a large group of zebras called?

_____

2. Why does a herd move from place to place?

_____

_____

3. What are some other animals that move in groups?

_____

4. Why do zebras' stripes make it hard for lions to catch a zebra?

_____

_____

5. How are a zebra's stripes similar to a human's fingerprints?

_____

6. What animals are a threat to zebras?

_____

7. In what part of the world are zebras found?

_____

8. A zebra's stripes are a form of camouflage. What is another animal that uses camouflage? Explain.

_____

_____

Some of these sentences are about **real** things. Write **R** by them. The other sentences are about **make believe** things. Write **M** by them.

1. _____ Houses are not on the ground.

2. _____ Children wear space suits.

3. _____ People look at old pictures.

4. What do you learn about Lorna from the picture?

_____

5. Why does Lorna ask about getting a car up to a house?

_____

6. Look at the picture. What do you like best about Lorna's world?

_____

7. Do you think Lorna lives in the past or in the future? Explain.

_____

_____

8. What is the setting for this story?

_____

9. Why do you think Lorna feels that having a house on the ground is weird?

_____

_____

10. In the photo, Lorna's great grandma is wearing a _____ .

One City Block

Read to see who lives on Rachel's block.

1 Mama says the whole world lives right here on our block. Everyone is different, and I'll always like it that way.

2 Right down the hall is Mrs. Rotollo. She and her husband speak Italian, but when they see me, they always say "hello" in English. When Mama was sick once, Mrs. Rotollo helped me make dinner. It turned out yummy!

3 Upstairs is Philip. He takes dancing lessons. When I hear his feet thumping in the morning, I know it is time to get up.

4 Next door is Mr. Tran's grocery. Mama sends me over for fresh vegetables and fruit. Mr. Tran always picks out the best ones for me.

5 On the first floor of our building is Mrs. Moya's shop. I love the colors! I always know when it's going to rain because she takes her piñatas down.

Write one thing you know about each of Rachel's neighbors.

1. Mr. and Mrs. Rotollo _____

2. Philip _____

3. Mr. Tran _____

4. Mrs. Moya _____

5. Look at the picture and the story. Which neighbor seems most interesting to you? Write why.

_____

6. In the picture, who is Rachel? How do you know?

_____

_____

7. Would you like to live in an apartment like Rachel's? Why or why not?

_____

_____

8. How does Rachel know it is time to get up in the morning?

_____

9. In the first paragraph, why does Mama say "the whole world lives right here on our block?"

_____

_____

What Is a City?

What kinds of people, buildings, and jobs make up your city?

1   A city is made up of people. They live and work in the city. Some of them work to make sure the city is a good place to live. They make rules for the people in the city. One rule might be, "Don't throw trash in the street." What rules does your city have?

2   Other people try to make sure there are things to do in a city. They run restaurants, movie theaters, and sports centers. The bigger a city is, the more things there are to do. What is there to do in your city?

3   If a city is going to be a nice place to live, the people who live there must agree to follow the city's rules. They must also pay taxes. Taxes pay for things such as cleaning the streets, running schools, and filling the public library with books. Is your city a nice place to live?

1. This article is mostly about

_____ what makes a city.   _____ how to live in a city.

_____ America's largest cities.

2. What is your favorite thing to do in your city or in a nearby city? Write about it.

_____

3. The person who wrote this article is the _____ .

4. Do you think this article is meant to give information or to make you laugh? Write why.

_____

5. Would you most like to live in a city, in a small town, or in the country? Explain.

_____

6. Which of the following would taxes NOT pay for?

_____ library books   _____ a new clothing store

_____ street cleaning

7. If you made the rules for a city, what rule would be most important to you?

_____

8. It is more fun to live in a city than in the country. Is this a fact or an opinion?

_____

Ant and Grasshopper

What does Grasshopper learn?

1   Ant hurried back and forth. Each time he went, he carried another small piece of food back to his nest. *I have to fill the nest, I have to fill the nest,* he panted to himself as he worked.

2   Grasshopper watched. He thought Ant was silly. "Come watch the bugs skate on the pond," he called to Ant.

3   Ant didn't even stop. "Oh, no, I can't. I must get more food for winter. I have to fill the nest."

4   So it went all summer. Grasshopper called out every day, and Ant answered the same.

5   When the leaves had all fallen off the trees, a sharp wind began to blow. Ant crawled safely into his nest. Grasshopper had nowhere to go.

6   In spring, when there were fresh green buds on the trees, Ant came out of his nest. Grasshopper was nowhere to be found.

Some of these sentences are about **real** things. Write **R** by them. The other sentences are about **make believe** things. Write **M** by them.

1. _____ Ants gather food.

2. _____ Grasshoppers watch baseball games.

3. _____ Grasshoppers are lazy.

4. This story is called a **fable**. Fables usually teach a lesson. What lesson does this one teach?

_____

_____

5. If you were Ant, what would you have said to Grasshopper?

_____

6. What makes Ant and Grasshopper different from real insects?

_____

7. What season is it when the story begins? What season is it when the story ends?

_____   _____

8. In paragraph 1, why do you think the words *I have to fill the nest* are in italics?

_____

9. Why does Grasshopper think Ant is silly?

_____

1. Most stories include a problem. What is this story's problem?

_____

2. As you began to read "Baxter's Shoes," who did you think Baxter was?

_____

3. The **narrator** is the person who tells a story. Whom does the narrator ask for help?

_____

4. What is Mom's rule about shoes?

_____

_____

5. Does this story seem realistic to you? Why or why not?

_____

_____

6. She never asked me where her shoes were. Is this a fact or an opinion?

_____

7. Do you think the boy in the story has lost his shoes before? Explain.

_____

8. What do you do when you have lost something at home?

_____

Getting Ready

How does Andrea get ready for the game?

1   Andrea's teacher, Mrs. McKay, was all excited. The yearly kickball game against Mr. Haskins' class was tomorrow. Andrea had an icky feeling in her stomach. She didn't know how to play kickball, and she wasn't sure she wanted to learn.

2   After Andrea came home from school, her mom could tell something was wrong. Andrea told her about the game.

3   "We can fix that," said Mom, opening the back door. "Welcome to the backyard kickball field." An hour later, Andrea had practiced pitching, kicking, fielding, and running the bases. She had won the game, even without any teammates. Mom had been a really good sport about it. Now, Andrea was ready for tomorrow!

Find words in the story with these meanings.

1. once every twelve months _____
(Par. 1)

2. find out, get information _____
(Par. 1)

3. area of open ground _____
(Par. 3)

4. Andrea is worried because _____ .

5. Put a check mark by the sentence that best tells about how Andrea looks in the picture.

_____ Andrea is working hard.   _____ Andrea is lazy.

_____ Andrea thinks kickball is funny.

6. What lesson did Andrea learn?

Things work out if

_____ you keep things to yourself.

_____ you let people help you.

_____ you never let anyone see you have a problem.

7. In the story, what is the solution to Andrea's problem?

_____

8. How do you think Andrea feels at the end of the story?

_____ grateful   _____ lonely   _____ stressed

9. How did Andrea's mom know something was wrong?

_____

Fitness for Life

How do you keep yourself healthy?

Healthful Lifestyle

1   Experts agree that a well-rounded healthful lifestyle is the best way to be healthy. You can't just watch what you eat. You can't just exercise. You have to eat well and exercise.

Eat well

2   Choose wisely from among the four food groups. These groups are fruit and vegetables, grains, dairy, and meat. Do not snack on sweet or salty foods between meals. Also, drink eight glasses of water a day.

Exercise

3   Exercising regularly at least three times each week is the best plan. If that's just not possible, at least be active. Use stairs instead of elevators. Walk the last few blocks to school or work. Take a walk instead of watching television. Make healthy choices.

1. What is this article mostly about?

_____ It is important to eat the right foods.

_____ Make sure you exercise every day.

_____ Eat well and exercise to stay healthy.

2. If people don't have time to exercise, what can they do to stay active? Write two ideas.

_____   _____

3. What do you do to stay healthy?

_____

4. For each pair of foods, circle the more healthful choice.

apple   crackers   chips   celery and peanut butter

yogurt   toaster pastry

5. Why is taking the stairs a better choice than the elevator?

_____

_____

6. What healthful snacks do you enjoy?

_____

7. Give one example of a food from each of the food groups.

fruits and vegetables _____   grains _____

dairy _____   meat _____

Snow Rooms

Read about a great snow day.

1 It was a magical day. I woke up and looked out the window. Everything was white. It had snowed a ton during the night. I didn't even have to ask about school. There was no way!

2 By 8 o'clock, my sister and I were outside. We went to the top of a little hill and jumped down. We knew there was a hollow under all that drifted snow. By pushing against the snow with our shoulders, we were able to widen our holes into spaces. Before long, the spaces became two rooms with a door between them.

3 We fixed up our rooms with snow benches, and I even made a snow picture on the wall. We lost all track of time. Mom finally came and got us. But first, she had some snow lunch with us in our snow rooms.

1. There was no school because _____

_____ .

2. The girls made rooms by _____

_____ .

3. The girls lost track of time, so _____ .

4. What did the girls add to their snow rooms?

_____

5. What did Mom do when she came to get the girls?

_____

Some of these sentences are about **real** things. Write **R** by them. The other sentences are about **make believe** things. Write **M** by them.

6. _____ Snowflakes are magic.

7. _____ Girls make snow forts.

8. _____ Snowmen come to life.

9. Who is the narrator of the story?

_____

10. How do you think the girls felt about their day?

_____ happy   _____ bored   _____ disappointed

11. What do you think the girls will do next?

_____

Wilson Bentley (1865-1931)

Read about the man who taught us about snowflakes.

1 You've heard the saying that "no two snowflakes are alike." How does anyone know this? We know because of the life and work of a quiet Vermont farmer who loved snow.

2 As a boy, Wilson Bentley was interested in many things. One thing he liked to do was look at objects under a microscope. He had the idea of looking at snowflakes, and he discovered how beautiful they were, and how different.

3 As Bentley got older, he wanted to show this beauty to others. He figured out a way to take a picture through a microscope. During the next 45 years, he took pictures of more than 5,000 snowflakes. Though he never made much money, "Snowflake" Bentley was always happy to share the beauty and the mystery of snowflakes with others.